Made by God
Insects

Primary

Published by In Celebration™
an imprint of

McGraw Hill **Children's Publishing**

Project Director: Alyson Kieda
Editor: Angella Phebus, Kim Bradford

McGraw Hill Children's Publishing

Published by In Celebration™
An imprint of McGraw-Hill Children's Publishing
Copyright © 2004 McGraw-Hill Children's Publishing

All Rights Reserved • Printed in the United States of America

Limited Reproduction Permission: Permission to duplicate these materials is limited to the person for whom they are purchased. Reproduction for an entire school or school district is unlawful and strictly prohibited.

Scripture is taken from the HOLY BIBLE: NEW INTERNATIONAL VERSION®. NIV®. Copyright © 1973, 1978, 1984 by International Bible Society. Used by permission of Zondervan Publishing House.

The "NIV" and "New International Version" trademarks are registered in the United States Patent and Trademark Office by International Bible Society.

Send all inquiries to:
McGraw-Hill Children's Publishing
3195 Wilson Drive NW
Grand Rapids, Michigan 49544

Made by God: Insects—primary
ISBN: 0-7424-2799-4

1 2 3 4 5 6 7 8 9 MAL 08 07 06 05 04

Table of Contents

The Wise Ant 4–5	The Singing Grasshopper ...19–20
What Do Ants Prefer? 6	Grasshopper Guided Discovery 21
The Swarming Bee 7–8	The Invading Locust............22–23
Insect Investigation 9	An Insect Hunt 24
The Biting Flea 10–11	The Consuming Moth..........25–26
Like a Kangaroo? 12	Metamorphosis 27
The Buzzing Fly 13–14	The Spinning Spider............28–29
A Better Fly Trap 15	A Web of Facts 30
The Annoying Gnat 16–17	Tangrams..................................31
What Do You Know About Gnats?.............18	Student Award 32

Introduction

This book offers what you need to teach 9 units on insects from a scientific and a biblical perspective. Included in each unit you will find two pages of teacher resources that include facts about each subject, a memory verse, Scripture links, bulletin board ideas, experiments, writing suggestions, arts and crafts, and more. The first page of every unit features facts, which can be used in many ways such as enlarging, cutting into strips, reading with students, and pasting to a bulletin board. Each unit is based on National Science Education Standards and includes a worksheet designed for the student.

The Wise Ant

Words from the Word

"Go to the ant, you sluggard; consider its ways and be wise! It has no commander, no overseer or ruler, yet it stores its provisions in summer and gathers its food at harvest" (Proverbs 6:6–8).

Fantastic Facts

- Ants live in groups or communities called **colonies**.
- An ant colony may have from a dozen to millions of members.
- A colony may have one or many queens.
- A queen may lay thousands of eggs in her lifetime.
- Most members of a colony are workers.
- Queens are usually several times larger than workers.
- All workers are females.
- Workers build nests, care for young, search for food, and fight enemies.
- The only job of the short-lived males is to mate with young queens.
- Males live only a few months or weeks until they mate and then die.
- Queens live from 10 to 20 years.
- Workers live from 1 to 5 years.
- There are about 20,000 species of ants.
- Ants may be grouped according to their way of life: army ants, slave makers, harvester ants, dairying ants, honey ants, and fungus growers.
- Ants live everywhere except extremely cold climates.
- Ants vary in size from more than an inch (2.5 cm) to 1/25 inch (0.1 cm) long.
- Ants are able to lift items that weigh as much as 50 times their body weight.
- Ants have a hard, shell-like covering called an **exoskeleton**, which protects their internal organs.
- Like all insects, ants have six legs and three main body parts—**head, trunk,** and **metasoma**.

Scripture Links

- Though ants are small, Solomon calls ants extremely wise (Proverbs 30:24–25).

Let's Explore!
An Ant Farm

Study a colony of ants by purchasing an ant farm. Many school supply and hobby stores sell the clear, plastic containers that house the ants and include a certificate you exchange for live ants. Place the ant farm in a center for close observation. Include magnifying glasses.

Another option is to construct your own ant farm. You will need cotton, soil, dark paper, cheesecloth, and a one-gallon jar with lid. Fill the jar halfway full with soil. Locate an anthill. Use a shovel to carefully lift the anthill and surrounding dirt and debris into the jar. Place some cotton on top of the dirt and moisten with water every few days. Cover the opening with cheesecloth. Secure closed. Poke tiny holes in the cheesecloth for air. Feed the ants crumbs of bread or cereal with honey. Cover the jar with dark paper to encourage the ants to make tunnels. Observe and discuss. Release after a few weeks.

The Wise Ant (cont.)

Helpful or Harmful?
Do research to learn how ants are both helpful and harmful. Some questions to consider include: How are ants helpful to farmers? How are ants harmful to crops? How are ants household pests? How are ants helpful in nature? Make a T-chart of the results.

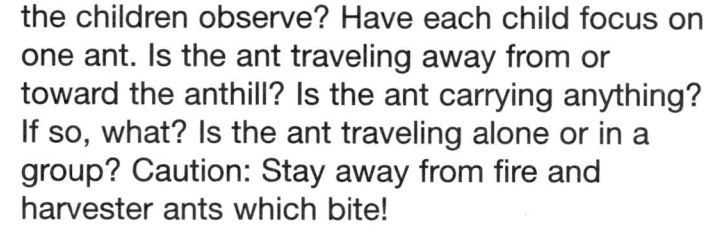

Are Ants Wise?
Read Proverbs 6:6–8 and 30:24–25. Discuss how ants are wise. What does this say about God? What can we learn from observing ants? Write a story about a wise ant.

Label the Parts
Enlarge and use the diagram below to label the three main parts of the ant's body. Have older children label the ant in more detail.

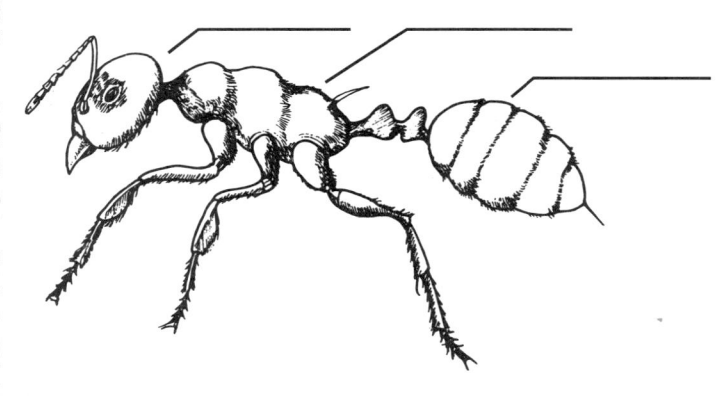

Field Trip
If weather allows, go outside and observe an active anthill. Larger groups may need to be divided up into groups of 3 or 4, and several nearby anthills will need to be located. What do the children observe? Have each child focus on one ant. Is the ant traveling away from or toward the anthill? Is the ant carrying anything? If so, what? Is the ant traveling alone or in a group? Caution: Stay away from fire and harvester ants which bite!

Ant Comparisons
Use the Internet to research and compare two different types of ants. Write a short report or make a poster to highlight each ant.

Ant Art
Let your students create their own ants. Provide art supplies such as Styrofoam balls, pipe cleaners, modeling clay, google eyes, toothpicks, markers, tempera paint, and scraps of fabric. Encourage children to design realistic bodies but to be as creative as they like. Display.

Anthills
Help students research anthills on the Internet or in other resources. Cut an anthill shape from brown butcher paper. Draw a series of tunnels and rooms on the anthill. Label each room according to its purpose and add details such as ants, eggs, and food. Hang the anthill on your wall.

Name _____

What Do Ants Prefer?

Materials needed:
sugar, unsweetened drink mix, salt, sunflower seeds (unsalted), 2 large index cards, pencil, chart

What to do:

1. Draw a line down the middle of both cards. Label the four halves: sugar, sunflower seeds, salt, and drink mix.

2. On the chart below, record your predictions about ant preferences.

3. Go outside and place the index cards side by side about three or four feet from an anthill.

4. Place a small amount of each ingredient in the correct spot on each card.

5. Observe the ants for five to ten minutes and record your observations.

Foods	Predictions	Observations
Sugar		
Sunflower Seeds		
Salt		
Unsweetened Drink Mix		

© McGraw-Hill Children's Publishing 0-7424-2799-4 *Made by God: Insects*

The Swarming Bee

Words from the Word

"In that day the LORD will whistle for flies from the distant streams of Egypt and for bees from the land of Assyria" (Isaiah 7:18).

Fantastic Facts

- Bees produce honey and beeswax.
- There are about 20,000 kinds of bees, but only honey bees make honey and beeswax in large enough quantities to be used by humans.
- Bees collect grains of pollen and a sweet liquid called **nectar** from blossoms. They make honey from the nectar and use both honey and pollen for food.
- Like most insects, bees have six legs and four wings.
- Bees fall into two main categories: solitary bees and social bees. Most bees are solitary bees and live alone.
- Like ants, social bees live in **colonies**, or communities.
- A honey bee colony includes one queen, thousands of workers, and a few hundred **drones**, which are the males.
- Honey bees live in **hives**, a storage space such as a box or hollow tree that contains a honeycomb.
- Worker bees have **stingers**, or stings, that they use to defend their home and their lives. Once a worker uses its sting, it dies.
- Laying eggs is the queen's only job. In the spring, a queen may lay as many as 2,000 eggs a day.
- The drones' job is to mate with queens. They depend on workers to feed them.
- Social bees include not only honey bees but also stingless bees and bumblebees.
- Solitary bees have no workers. Each bee is like a queen that does its own work.
- Types of solitary bees include the carpenter, leaf-cutting, miner, cuckoo, and mason bees.
- When an old queen and many workers leave an overcrowded hive, their flight is called **swarming**.

Scripture Links

- When the Israelites rebelled against the Lord, the Amorites chased them like a swarm of bees (Deuteronomy 1:43–44).
- After killing a lion, Samson returned to find it covered by honey and a swarm of bees (Judges 14:5–9).
- Nations are compared to swarming bees (Psalm 118:10–12).

Let's Explore!
Tongue Twisters

Using alliteration, write a tongue twister about bees such as: Busy bees buzz by baby bears. Write it on a board. Read it together and then allow several children to try to say it out loud. Write another tongue twister with the class. Then allow the children to write and illustrate their own tongue twister about bees or an insect of their choice. Display on a bulletin board.

The Swarming Bee (cont.)

Bees and Ants
Use a Venn diagram to compare honey bees and ants.

A Day in the Life
After learning about bees, have students write about a day in the life of a worker bee from the bee's perspective.

Class Visitor
Invite a beekeeper to visit and speak with your class. Encourage the beekeeper to bring in a honeycomb and wear beekeeping attire. Afterwards, be sure to have your class write thank you notes to your visitor.

Honey and Beeswax
Bring in foods that include honey as an ingredient (such as crackers and cold medicines) and items that contain beeswax (such as candles, lipstick, and polishes). Or cut out pictures of these items from magazines or newspapers. Place in a center. Encourage students to create a poster or bulletin board on the usefulness of the bee.

Why Do Flowers Need Bees?
Have advanced students research and write reports on pollination using the Internet and other sources. Encourage students to present their reports to the class.

The Honey Bee Dance
Worker bees called scouts dance a figure-8 pattern up the honeycomb to indicate where distant nectar is located. The faster the bee dances, the nearer the food is located. The imaginary line between the loops shows the position of the nectar in relation to the sun. Try hiding a flower in the room. Have someone move in a figure-8 and have the class guess if the flower is near or far. Another option is to attach a picture of a bee to a craft stick and have students do the dance to show classmates the location of their flowers.

Learn and Draw
Learn about one of the solitary bees listed in the Fantastic Facts. Write a few facts about it and draw its nest. Put together in a class book about bees. Children also may enjoy making a model of a bee's nest.

Name_____

Insect Investigation

Insects usually have three pairs of legs, three body parts, and two sets of wings. Choose a bee or other insect to investigate. Look on the Internet, in encyclopedias, or in books to find out about your insect. Answer the questions below and then draw an illustration.

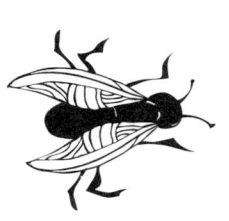

1. What is the name of your insect? _____

2. Describe what it looks like.

   _____
   _____

3. Where does it live?

   _____
   _____

4. How does it move? _____

5. What does it eat? _____

6. What are some other interesting facts about your insect?

   _____

7. Draw a picture of your insect.

The Biting Flea

Words from the Word
"The king of Israel has come out to look for a flea—as one hunts a partridge in the mountains" (1 Samuel 26:20).

Fantastic Facts
- The flea is a tiny, wingless insect that lives on the blood of birds and mammals.
- In biblical times, fleas were pests just as they are today.
- Fleas are dangerous pests because they can carry the germs that cause such diseases as typhus and plague.
- Fleas pick up germs by biting infected ground squirrels and rats.
- Fleas live on cats, dogs, birds, rats, horses, poultry, rabbits, and many wild animals, as well as humans.
- Most fleas can pass from one animal to another but cannot live on dead animals.
- A flea's head is much smaller than the rest of its flat, oblong body.
- A flea's shape and its strong, spiny legs help it move easily and quickly through the hairs or feathers of its host.
- Fleas use their sharp jaws to puncture the skin.
- A flea bite is painful and can cause swelling and itching.
- Fleas have unusual jumping ability for their small size and have been observed to leap 13 inches (33 cm).
- The human, or European, flea is about 1/8 inch (3 mm) long.
- The common flea lives in the folds of clothing and drops its eggs around the house.
- Another type of flea, the chigoe, is native to South America but has spread to Africa and other warm areas.
- The best protection against fleas is cleanliness and the proper care of pets.

Scripture Links
- David spares Saul's life when Saul enters the cave where David and his men are hiding. David asks Saul, "Whom are you pursuing? A dead dog? A flea?" (1 Samuel 24:14).

Let's Explore!
Magnified Flea
Set up a microscope in a center so that each student has a chance to get a magnified view of a flea. Some microscopes come with prepared slides, and may already include a flea. If not, prepared slides may be purchased individually. Have each student draw and label a detailed picture of the flea.

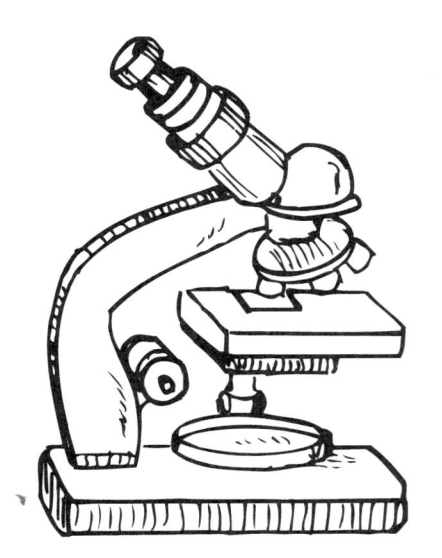

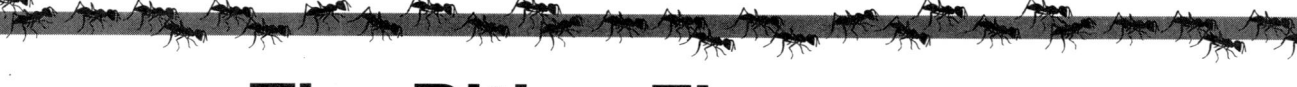

The Biting Flea (cont.)

Flea Cinquains

Provide the pattern and then write a cinquain poem with your class. Line 1: noun; line 2: two adjectives; line 3: three verbs; line 4: four-word statement about noun; line 5: repeat noun or use a synonym of noun. **Example:**

Flea
Tiny, strong
Jumping, biting, sucking
Small carrier of disease
Pest

Flea Circus

Fleas have been trained to pull miniature wagons. Flea circuses feature fleas that have been trained to perform these and other tricks. Pretend you are the owner of a flea circus. What tricks will your fleas perform? Write a program that lists each of these amazing tricks. Then put on a flea circus. Copy, color, and attach the flea pattern below to a craft stick. Use your flea to pull a wagon, leap through a ring, or perform another trick of your choice.

Visit a Veterinarian

As a class, visit a vet or invite a vet to your classroom. Learn about proper pet care. Be sure the vet covers what can be done to keep your pet and home free from fleas. Write thank you notes when you return to class.

Compound Eyes

Explain that many insects have compound eyes. Their eyes have lenses that capture many small pictures at the same time. The small pictures are put together before they go to the insect's brain so a whole picture is seen. Have students draw a picture of their house on an 8 1/2" x 11" piece of white construction paper. Encourage students to use all of the white space and to include many details. Discuss the similarities and differences between how insects and people see. Have students cut their pictures into pieces, mix them up, and then put them back together to act out how an insect's eyes work. For further exploration, have students draw the home of an insect and follow the steps above. Then compare the two pictures and talk about different places people and insects live. Discuss how they are similar and different.

Sing a Round

Use the tune of "Frere Jacques" to make up a song about fleas or another insect.
Example:
I see a dog,
I see a dog,
Scratching a flea,
Scratching a flea,
Stay away from me, flea,
Stay away from me, flea.
Hop away.
Hop away.

Now have students make up words to fit another well-known round, such as "Row, Row, Row Your Boat." Encourage creativity and include flea facts.

© McGraw-Hill Children's Publishing

0-7424-2799-4 *Made by God: Insects*

Name _____

Like a Kangaroo?

Fill in the lines below and use your information in the Venn diagram. You may compare yourself to a flea or a flea to a kangaroo.

1. List ways a flea is like a kangaroo. _____
   _____

2. List ways a flea is different from a kangaroo. _____
   _____

3. List ways you are like a flea. _____
   _____

4. List ways you are different from a flea. _____
   _____

Extra: Using a word processing system, write a paragraph telling why you are glad God made you a person and not a flea. Then use your computer's drawing program to create a self-portrait.

The Buzzing Fly

Words from the Word
"As dead flies give perfume a bad smell, so a little folly outweighs wisdom and honor" (Ecclesiastes 10:1).

Fantastic Facts
- There are about 100,000 types of flies.
- One of the best known flies is the common house fly. This fly is common to the Holy Land.
- Other flies include black flies, deer flies, fruit flies, gnats, midges, sand flies, and mosquitoes.
- Flies have two wings. Many other insects called flies are not true flies because they have four wings. These include dragonflies and mayflies.
- Flies can be dangerous pests because they carry germs that cause diseases such as malaria, dysentery, and sleeping sickness.
- Some flies are helpful because they carry pollen from one plant to another.
- Flies are among the fastest flying insects. A fly's buzz is the sound of its beating wings.
- A house fly's wings beat about 200 times a second, while some midge's wings beat as many as 1,000 times a second.
- The fly has one set of wings and three main body parts: the **head, thorax,** and **abdomen**.
- Flies have two large **compound eyes** that cover much of its head. Compound eyes contain thousands of six-sided lenses.
- A fly has four stages of life: **egg, larva, pupa,** and **adult**.
- Different species of fly lay from one to around 250 eggs at a time.
- A fly's larva is often called a **maggot**. It lives in garbage, food, sewage, soil, and both living and dead plants and animals.
- Adult house flies live about 21 days in the summer and longer in the winter.
- Most flies die in the winter but a few hibernate. Many pupae and larvae stay alive during the winter and become adults in the spring.

Scripture Links
- God sent a plague of flies on the people of Egypt (Exodus 8:20–32; Psalm 78:45).
- When God spoke, swarms of flies appeared (Psalm 105:31).
- In the day of the Lord, God "will whistle for flies from the distant streams of Egypt" (Isaiah 7:18).

Let's Explore!
Shoe Flies
Make your own "shoe flies." On 9" x 12" sheets of white paper, trace the sole of a child's shoe. Draw the tread design inside the outline. Then draw additional body parts such as antennae, legs, wings, and eyes. Color and cut out to display.

The Buzzing Fly (cont.)

Metamorphosis
What is metamorphosis? Scientists use this term to describe the extreme changes in appearance that occur in animals such as flies, beetles, ants, and bees. Discuss this process with children using the fly as an example. Show illustrations of the life cycle of the fly. Have students write a description of the fly's life cycle.

Class Survey
Conduct a class survey. Ask, "What is your least favorite fly and why?" If desired, limit options to house fly, mosquito, deer fly, fruit fly, and gnat. Record results in a bar graph. For a homework assignment, have students survey 10 family members or friends and then graph results.

Least Favorite Fly

	house fly	mosquito	deer fly	fruit fly	gnat
10					
9					
8					
7					
6					
5					
4					
3					
2					
1					

What Rhymes with Fly?
Brainstorm a list of words that rhyme with fly and have children use these words to create a three- to six-line rhyming poem. Have children illustrate their poems and bind the poems together into a class book. Read again and again for enjoyment and to instill the love of reading.

Example:
Oh, no, could it be a fly I spy?
Whenever I hear a fly, I sigh.
Nothing bothers me more than a fly.

Fly Fact or Fiction?
Call out statements about flies. Use the Fantastic Facts and whatever else you know to be true or false about flies. Ask children to stand if they think a statement is true and stay seated if they think the statement is false. Make into a game by eliminating those with incorrect guesses until only one student remains. For added fun, give statements about more than one type of insect.

Insect Investigations
Take a class field trip to a nearby field or park. Find a good place to sit and observe insects. Ask questions such as: What insects do you see? What insects do you hear? How do different insect bodies compare? How are the insects similar and different? How do insects move? Instruct children to take notes and write down their observations and/or sketches of the insects they observe.

Name_____

A Better Fly Trap

Discuss fly traps and the essential elements needed, such as bait, an opening, and a difficult escape route. Then build a trap as a class or in small groups.

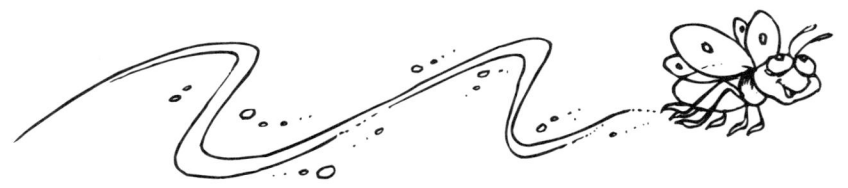

Materials needed:
half gallon (2 liter) cardboard milk container for each group, scissors, string, masking tape, small piece of raw meat, black construction paper, black spray paint

Teacher directions:
- Cut off the bottom of the milk cartons.
- Spray the insides of the cartons with black paint and allow to dry overnight.
- Make sure the students wash hands after handling the meat.

Class or group directions:
1. Tie a small piece of meat on a string.
2. Poke a small hole in the top of the carton and thread the string up through the hole so the meat lands inside the carton near the top.
3. Tape the other end of the string to the outside of the carton, and cover the hole with tape.
4. Cut a 1" (2.5 cm) square at the base of the carton to allow in flies.
5. Cover the bottom of the carton with black construction paper and tape in place.
6. Place the fly trap(s) in various locations in or outside the classroom. Observe.

Complete the following questions together or individually.

7. What attracted the flies to the traps? _____

8. What made the flies stay in the traps? _____

_____

The Annoying Gnat

Words from the Word
"You blind guides! You strain out a gnat but swallow a camel" (Matthew 23:24).

Fantastic Facts
- Gnat is the name of a variety of small flies. Some types of gnats bite and feed on the blood of humans and animals.
- In biblical times, gnats would get into water and wine jugs and people would need to strain out the gnats before they could drink.
- Some gnats, such as black flies, lay their eggs on water and spread a disease called river blindness, which may cause blindness.
- Other types of gnats, such as fungus and wood gnats, lay eggs in moist or decaying plant foliage and in mushroom gardens.
- Gnats called punkies or no-see-ums lay eggs in or near mud, wet plant debris, and sand. These gnats have a nasty bite and are serious pests in the United States.
- The Hessian fly is a type of gnat that is harmful to wheat. This gnat lays its eggs in plant tissue.
- Fruit flies are a type of nonbiting gnat.

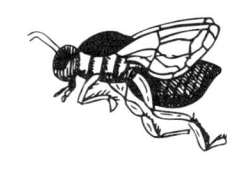

Scripture Links
- God sent a plague of gnats on the Egyptians (Exodus 8:16–19; Psalm 105:31).

Let's Explore!
The Plagues
Name the ten plagues found in Exodus 7–11. Note that several of the plagues were insects. Discuss how insects can be harmful and the impact they must have had on Egyptian daily life.

Gnat Snacks
Create tasty snacks shaped like gnats or other bugs. Supply children with a variety of items to choose from: mini marshmallows, thin licorice, oval-shaped fruit snacks, rolled-up fruit snacks, raisins, and grapes. Also supply toothpicks and/or frosting to hold the body parts together. Display for all to see and then enjoy your tasty treats.

A Food Chain
Discuss food chains. Have children create a food chain that includes gnats, frogs, fish, and humans.

Just Flying By
As a class, research and read about how and why insects fly. Next, sit with students in a circle and have them imagine they are a gnat flying with some gnat friends. Start a class gnat story by writing the first few sentences on chart paper. As you write, read your sentences aloud. Talk about what you wrote and why. Then beginning with the student seated on your left, ask each student to add a sentence or two to the story. Tell them to include details relating to the five senses and facts about how and why insects fly. Write each student's contribution to the story on the paper. Remind students to pay attention to what is already written to be sure their part makes sense. Also, guide students to include a beginning, middle, and an end. Frequently reread the story aloud to ensure a cohesive and flowing story. A variation is to write each student's contribution on a separate sheet of paper and later have them illustrate

The Annoying Gnat (cont.)

their part. The pages can then be put together as a class book for repeated reading enjoyment.

Number Poems

Instruct children to write each numeral in their telephone numbers down the left side of a sheet of paper. On the right side of the paper, have them write down the names of seven different insects. Then suggest they make the poems more interesting by adding adjectives. Finally, have the students illustrate their poems. Hang to display.

Example:
- 6 nasty gnats
- 7 leaping fleas
- 8 hopping grasshoppers
- 3 busy ants
- 4 buzzing flies
- 5 chewing locusts
- 1 pretty moth

Extension: Choose one of the insects from the poem, research on the Internet, and write a report.

Compare and Contrast

Have children use a Venn diagram to compare and contrast a gnat with another insect of their choice.

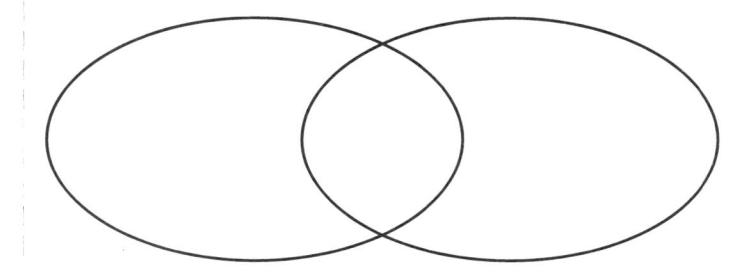

"Fly, Fly, Gnat"

Play a variation of the game "Duck, Duck, Goose." In this game, once the "Gnat" has made it home, he or she must give an insect fact in order to be truly safe.

Insect Trading Cards

Use the Fantastic Facts found in this book and facts from other sources to create trading cards. Give each student several blank 3" x 5" index cards. For each insect have students include a sketch or picture of the insect and the following:

Name:
Habitat:
What It Eats:
Enemies:
Interesting Facts:

Have the students share their cards with their friends. Then put the cards together in a class book or file in a recipe box and place in a center on insects.

Invent an Insect

As a class, have students list all of the attributes and characteristics they have learned about insects. Ask students to pretend they are entomologists who have discovered new kinds of insects. Have each student use the brainstormed list of attributes to create a detailed drawing of the new insect they invented.

© McGraw-Hill Children's Publishing

0-7424-2799-4 Made by God: Insects

Name _____

What Do You Know About Gnats?

Complete the web to show what you have learned about gnats.

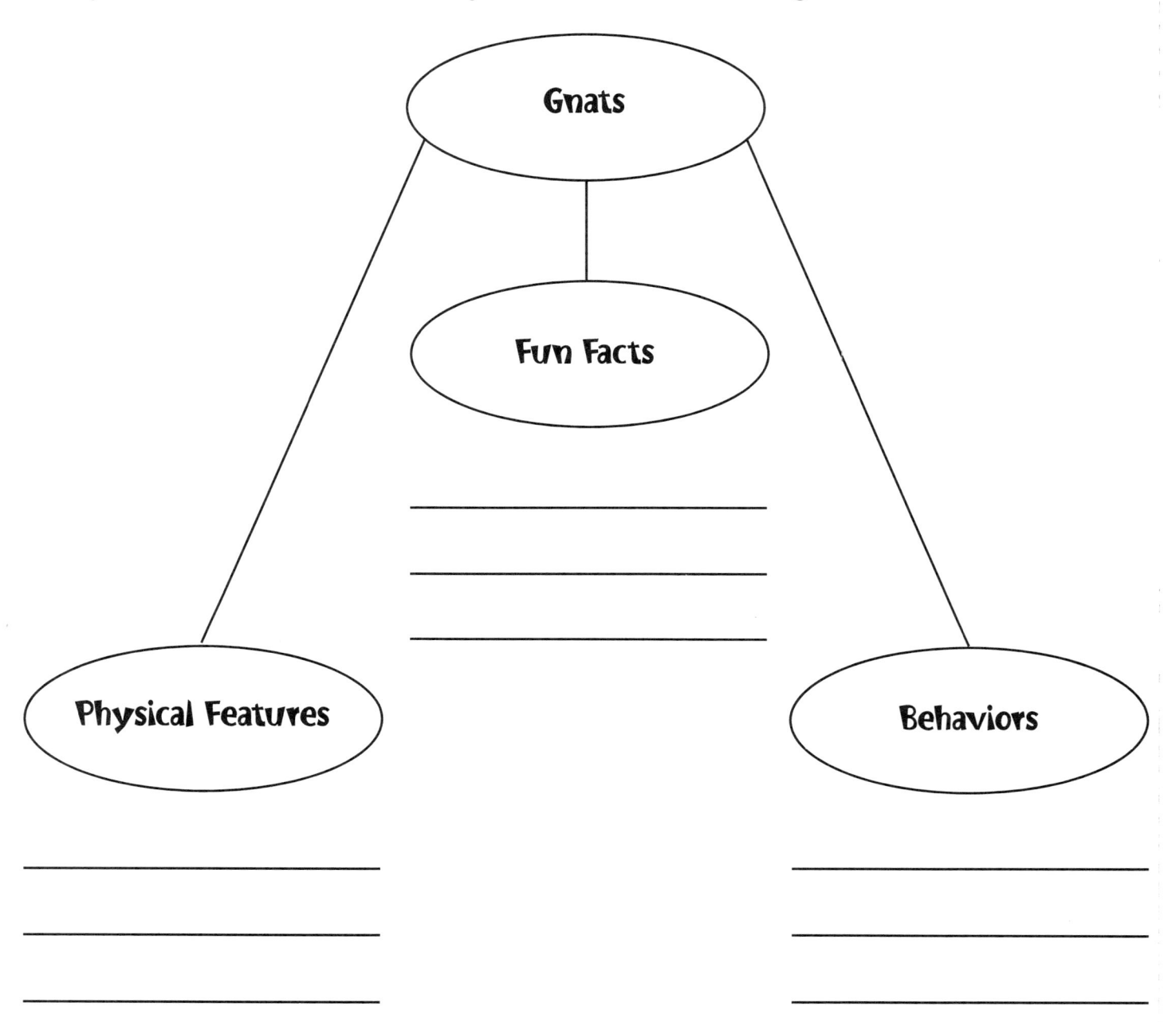

```
        ( Gnats )
       /   |    \
       |   |     \
       | (Fun Facts)
       |   |      \
       |  ___     \
       |  ___      \
       |  ___      \
(Physical Features)  (Behaviors)
  ___              ___
  ___              ___
  ___              ___
```

Extension:
On a separate sheet of paper, write a fictional story about gnats. Include facts and details you used in your web.

The Singing Grasshopper

Words from the Word

"He sits enthroned above the circle of the earth, and its people are like grasshoppers" (Isaiah 40:22).

🐞 Fantastic Facts

- Grasshoppers live in all areas of the world except the polar regions.
- A grasshopper can leap as much as 20 times as far as its body length.
- Grasshoppers are either long-horned with long **antennae** (feelers) or short-horned with short feelers.
- Like most insects, a grasshopper is covered with an **exoskeleton** and has three body parts—the **head, thorax,** and **abdomen.**
- Short-horned grasshoppers live in meadows and fields and eat plants. Some eat whatever is available, while others destroy whole fields of cotton, alfalfa, and other grains.
- The majority of long-horned grasshoppers eat plants, but some eat animal remains or other insects.
- Grasshoppers often escape their many enemies by jumping up and flying away, by hiding, or by biting with their strong jaws.
- Grasshoppers are **camouflaged**. This means their bodies blend in with their surroundings so that enemies do not see them unless they move.
- Most grasshoppers lay their eggs beginning in the late summer and into the fall. The eggs hatch in the spring. From 20 to 120 eggs are laid at one time
- Young grasshoppers look like adult grasshoppers but lack wings.
- It takes 40 to 60 days for a young grasshopper to become an adult. During this time, the grasshopper sheds its exoskeleton five or six times. This is called **molting**. After the last molt, the grasshopper has wings.
- Short-horned grasshoppers include migratory locusts and lubber grasshoppers.
- Long-horned grasshoppers include Mormon crickets and katydids.
- Male grasshoppers rub their wings together to produce sounds that attract females.

🐞 Scripture Links

- God told the Israelites that grasshoppers were an acceptable food (Leviticus 11:20–23).
- When the Israelite spies returned from exploring the land of Canaan, they reported that the people were of great size and that the Israelites seemed like grasshoppers in comparison (Numbers 13:31–33).
- Solomon asked God in prayer to hear his people when grasshoppers or other disasters afflicted them (1 Kings 8:37–39; 2 Chronicles 6:28–30).
- God destroyed the Egyptians' crops with grasshoppers (Psalm 78:46).
- We are called to remember God before we are so old that we are like grasshoppers that drag themselves along (Ecclesiastes 12:1–5).

The Singing Grasshopper (cont.)

🐞 Let's Explore!

Grasshopper Haikus

Have children create haikus about grasshoppers or another insect of their choice. Remind children that a haiku is a three-lined, unrhymed poem with a special pattern: lines one and three have five syllables, and line two has seven syllables. See the example below.

> High-leaping insect
> Makes loud music with its wings—
> Grasshopper love song.

Jump Like a Grasshopper

Some grasshoppers can jump 20 times their body length. Go outside and watch closely as a grasshopper jumps. Then have your students practice jumping and feeling their muscles expand and contract by doing a standard broad jump. Mark a line on the floor with a piece of tape or a line of chalk. Place both feet on the line and then jump as far as you can. Have each child try this movement. Use a yardstick or meter stick to measure the distance. Then measure a child and mark off 20 times that length to see how far a grasshopper could jump if it were as big as a student.

A Grasshopper's Enemies

Research and write a short paragraph about one of the grasshopper's enemies. If possible, draw a picture of the enemy using your computer's drawing program.

A Grasshopper's Song

If possible, listen to a tape of grasshoppers "singing." Then go outside and listen. Ask your students what they hear. Do they hear crickets? Katydids?

"Who Am I?"

Play "Who Am I?" using statements found in the Fantastic Facts. Research and add clues that pertain to a specific type of grasshopper such as a cricket or katydid. Some sample clues include:

> I am an animal.
> I am an insect.
> I can jump 20 times my body length.

Innovative Insects

Provide scrap material, construction material, ribbon, yarn, glitter, sequins, scissors, glue, and other items to create insects. Encourage children to be as innovative as they like but to be sure to include the correct number of body parts, legs, wings, and so on. Hang from the ceiling or use in a mobile.

Label the Parts

Enlarge the grasshopper below. Have children label the parts. For younger children include the following words written on cards: legs, antennae, eye, wings, head, thorax, and abdomen. Instruct them to label the parts by attaching the cards to the picture.

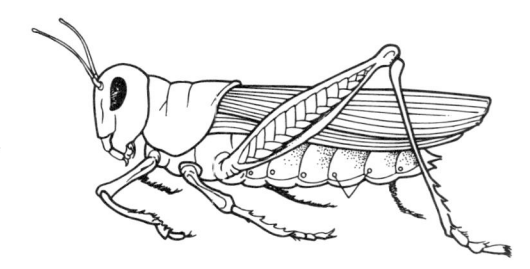

Name_____

Grasshopper Guided Discovery

Materials needed:
cricket or other grasshopper, magnifying glass, clear container with holes in lid, potato slice, colored pencils, metric ruler

What to do:
1. Place the cricket in the refrigerator for one hour.
2. While your cricket is cold and slow-moving, draw and color your cricket in the box.

[ ]

3. Label the head, thorax, abdomen, wings, antennae, and legs.

4. Measure your cricket's body.

   Length: _____ cm _____ mm

   Width: _____ cm _____ mm

5. Measure one antenna.

   _____ cm _____ mm

6. Is the antenna shorter, longer, or the same length as the cricket's body?

   _____

7. Use your magnifying glass to carefully study the cricket's wing. Draw what you see.

[ ]

8. Place the cricket in the container and watch for five minutes. Write what the cricket does.

   _____

   _____

   _____

   _____

© McGraw-Hill Children's Publishing   0-7424-2799-4 *Made by God: Insects*

The Invading Locust

Words from the Word
"Locusts have no king, yet they advance together in ranks" (Proverbs 30:27).

🪲 Fantastic Facts

- The locust is a type of grasshopper.
- Locusts are one of the most frequently mentioned insects in the Bible.
- The name **locust** can refer to any short-horned grasshopper, or grasshopper with short feelers.
- Locust most often refers to short-horned grasshoppers that **migrate**. This includes nine types.
- Every continent except Antarctica has migratory locusts.
- Most migratory locusts measure about 2 inches (5 cm) long and have a large head and short feelers.
- The reason for the migration of locusts is not fully understood. Scientists do know that migration takes place only after a great number of females lay eggs close together. This may result from local flooding or a food shortage.
- The young locusts that hatch from eggs laid close together live as a group. This group may meet other groups and form a **swarm**, which can include billions of insects.
- A swarm may fly long distances. Whenever they land, they devour and destroy vegetation. Eventually, the swarm is separated. Many generations of solitary locusts may result until conditions are once again right to create a swarm.
- Plagues of crop-destroying locusts have been known since ancient times.
- Locusts have destroyed millions of dollars worth of crops.
- Swarms are sometimes so huge that they block out the sunlight.
- Locusts are still a major problem, especially in east Africa.

🪲 Scripture Links

- Solomon mentioned locusts in a prayer (1 Kings 8:37; 2 Chronicles 6:28–30).
- God sent a plague of locusts (Exodus 10:1–20; Psalm 78:46).
- Invading people are compared to a swarm of locusts (Isaiah 33:4; Joel 1:4–6; 2:25).
- John the Baptist ate locusts and wild honey (Matthew 3:4).
- After the seventh seal is broken, an invasion of locusts arises (Revelation 9:1–11).

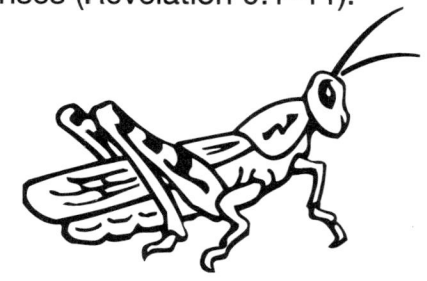

🪲 Let's Explore!
Insect Collages

Have students make creative collages about insects and their habitats. Provide nature magazines and other materials to use in the collages. Have students write or dictate about their collages. Display on a bulletin board.

The Invading Locusts (cont.)

Shape Stories
Provide paper outlines of locusts or other insects and have children write stories or poems about that insect. Give older students several copies and use one copy to create a cover. Display on a bulletin board or bind together into books and display in a center.

Insect Cage
Make an insect cage to keep and observe insects. Roll copper wire screen to fit two aluminum cake pans. Join the edges of the screen by sewing them together with a single strand of copper wire removed from the cut edge. Add the cake pans to form the top and bottom of the cage. Line the bottom of the cage with dirt, grass, and leaves. Capture insects and observe. After a few days, release your insects.

Locust Documentary
Use a camcorder to record a short documentary on locusts. Write a script focusing on a special ability or other cool fact about locusts and how we can see God's greatness through all his creation, including locusts.

Insect Poster
Create a poster about the locust or another insect covered in this book. Include an illustration or photo with details about its habitat, habits, diet, and characteristics. Work as a class or in small groups.

Class Visitor
Invite a farmer or scientist to come into the classroom and discuss ways to fight locusts and other insect pests. Send thank you notes to your visitor.

Class Book
Use the facts on page 22 to create a book. Have children rewrite and illustrate the facts. If desired, have children do further research, writing and illustrating other facts. Combine together in a class book. Have children use to quiz each other.

Puppet Play
Make realistic-looking locusts out of construction paper or cardstock. Cut them out and attach large craft sticks to use as puppets. Talk about how and when locusts swarm and explain that scientists don't know why they do so. Have students act out a swarm with their puppets and then tell or write their opinions of why they think locusts swarm.

Hatching Locusts
Collect locust or grasshopper eggs. Place the eggs in a clear container and observe. Talk about the life cycle of the locust. Watch the eggs hatch. Then catch a locust or grasshopper. Ask students to use their five senses to tell about the eggs hatching and to describe the adult. Ask questions such as: What do you see? How does it feel? What do you hear?

© McGraw-Hill Children's Publishing

0-7424-2799-4 *Made by God: Insects*

Name _____

An Insect Hunt

Go for a walk outside. Look and listen for the insects below. Draw and describe what you find.

A tiny insect	A loud insect
An insect that blends in with its surroundings	**An insect that can do something you cannot do**
A flying insect	**A busy insect**

The Consuming Moth

Words from the Word

"Do not store up for yourselves treasures on earth, where moth and rust destroy and where thieves break in and steal" (Matthew 6:19).

Fantastic Facts

- Moths are closely related to butterflies.
- Most moths and all butterflies have two pairs of wings—large front wings and smaller hind wings.
- The wings of moths and butterflies are covered with fine, powdery scales.
- Both moths and butterflies go through the same life cycle: from **egg**, to **larva** (caterpillar), to **pupa**, to **adult**.
- Moths live all over the world except in oceans.
- The size of moths varies greatly. The smallest moths have a wingspread of about 1/8 inch (0.3 cm), and the largest have a wingspread of up to 12 inches (30 cm). The smallest are called leafminers.
- Most moths fly at night or dusk, while most butterflies fly during the day.
- On most moths, the hind wing is attached to the front wing by a hook or set of hooks called a **frenulum**. Butterflies lack this.
- The **antennae**, or feelers, of most moths are not club-shaped like a butterfly's feelers.
- Adult moths feed mostly on nectar, while most caterpillars eat leaves and other plant parts.
- Some moth caterpillars eat clothing and other materials made of wool.
- The clothes moth of the Holy Land enters dwellings in the evening and lays eggs. A week later, the larvae hatch and consume anything made of animal fibers.
- In China, the cocoons of a certain species of moth are unraveled to produce silk.
- Moths are also important in the pollination of certain flowers.
- There are over 100,000 types of moths.

Scripture Links

- Man wastes away like a garment eaten by moths (Job 13:28).
- God disciplines men for their sins and consumes their wealth like a moth (Psalm 39:11).
- Those who falsely accuse the righteous will be eaten, or destroyed, by moths (Isaiah 50:9; 51:7–8).
- We are to build a treasure in heaven that cannot be destroyed by moth or thieves (Luke 12:33-34).

Let's Explore!
What's the Difference?

How are moths similar to butterflies? How are they different? Draw and label a picture to detail your answers. Show your results in a T-chart or Venn diagram.

Field Trip

Visit a museum or nature center to view moths and caterpillars, or invite an entomologist to bring in his/her collection and talk to the class.

© McGraw-Hill Children's Publishing

0-7424-2799-4 *Made by God: Insects*

The Consuming Moth (cont.)

Moth Alliteration
Brainstorm and write down words that begin with the letter M and could be used to describe moths. Create a moth pattern for each student. On the pattern, have students use the list or their own words to write and illustrate an alliterative sentence about moths. Have younger children think of a descriptive name for a moth such as material-munching moth.

Internet Explorers
Guide your children to safe sites that include pictures and information on moths. Provide a list of questions for your children to answer during their exploration.

A Moth's Life
Use information gathered in the activity "Internet Explorers" to write a story from the perspective of a moth that describes the moth's life cycle. Include details about each stage, diet, behavior, and so on. If desired, have students write their stories from the perspective of a caterpillar.

Life Cycle Models
Create life cycle models. Make an egg by placing a tiny ball of clay on a real or paper leaf or stick. Form caterpillars out of green or brown modeling clay or dough. Wrap a peanut shell with brown or green yarn to represent the cocoon. For a model of the adult moth, slip two pieces of tissue paper into a clothespin. Add eyes with a marker and attach a pipe cleaner for antennae.

Stained-Glass Moths
Follow the directions to create a window decoration. Adults will need to perform step 4. Note: Sizes may vary depending on enlargement size.

1. Copy, enlarge, and cut out the moth and frame pattern below.
2. Rub peeled crayons over a grater to make shavings of different colors.
3. Sprinkle the shavings evenly between the layers of a horizontally folded 9" x 12" piece of waxed paper.
4. Place the folded sheet of waxed paper on a thick layer of newspaper. Cover with another piece of newspaper. Press with a warm iron until the shavings melt and blend. Carefully remove and let cool.
5. Fold a 9" x 12" sheet of black construction paper vertically.
6. Center the pattern on the folded black paper. Trace around the moth and the inside of the frame. Cut through both thicknesses of paper.
7. Place the waxed paper between the folded frame and staple in place.

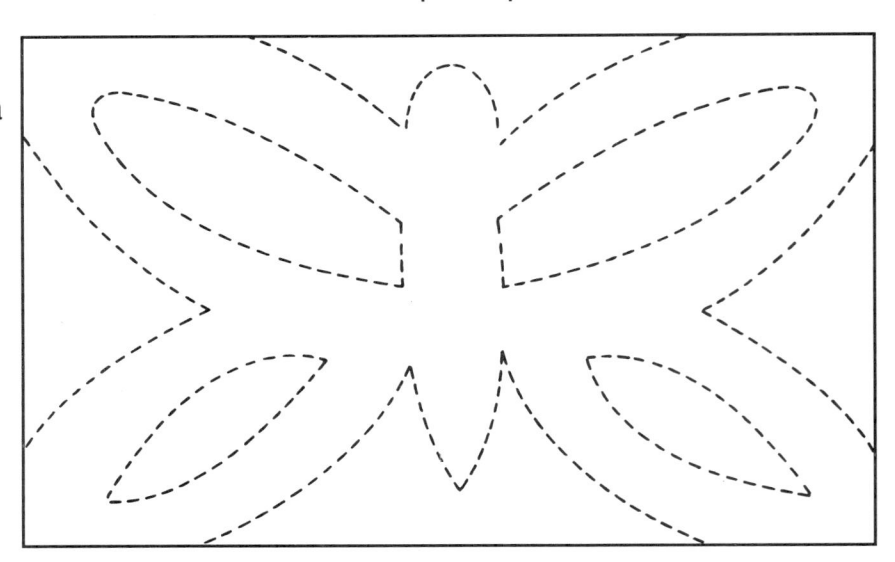

Name _____

Metamorphosis

Use the words in the Word Bank. Label the life cycle of a moth.

Word Bank
adult   egg   pupa   larva

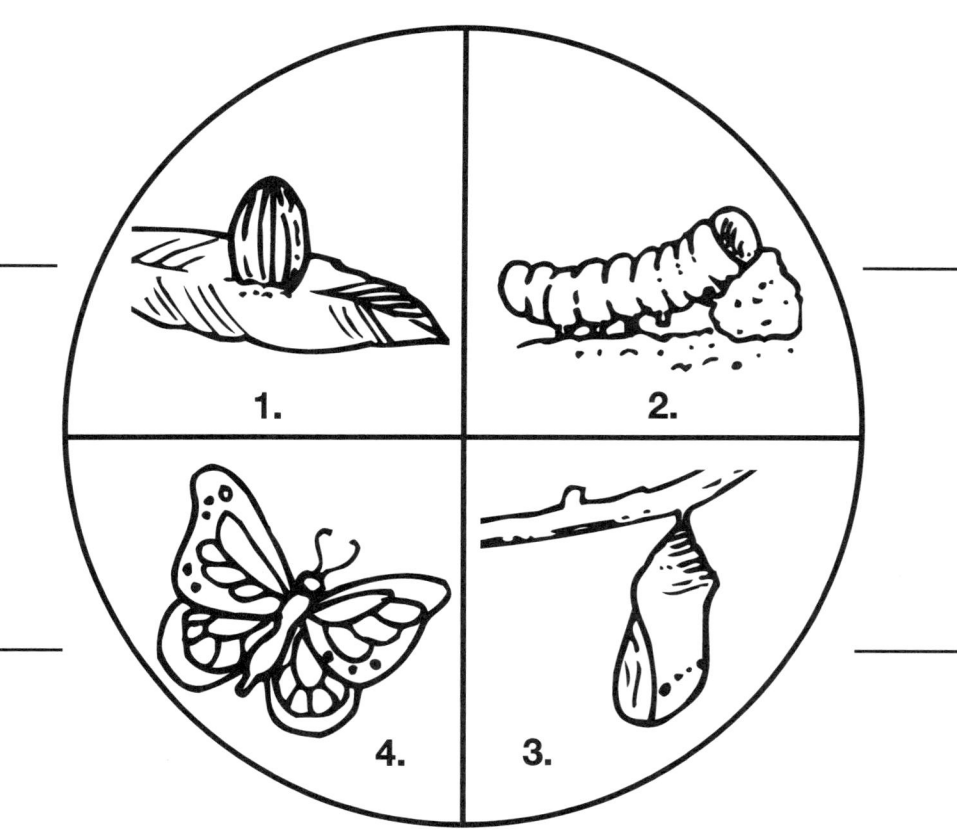

1. _____
2. _____
3. _____
4. _____

Write two fun facts about moths.

_____
_____
_____
_____

The Spinning Spider

Words from the Word
"Such is the destiny of all who forget God; so perishes the hope of the godless. What he trusts in is fragile; what he relies on is a spider's web. He leans on his web, but it gives way; he clings to it, but it does not hold" (Job 8:13–15).

Fantastic Facts
- Spiders are not insects. They are part of the **arachnid** family.
- Other arachnids include scorpions, ticks, and daddy longlegs.
- Unlike insects, spiders have eight legs and lack wings.
- A spider's body has two main sections, whereas an insect's body has three.
- All spiders spin silk, but not all spin webs.
- All spiders have **fangs**, and most have **poison glands**. These are used for capturing animals for food.
- Only a few types of spiders are harmful to humans.
- Spiders are helpful to humans because they eat harmful insects such as locusts and mosquitoes.
- Most spiders rely on a diet of insects, but some eat small fish and frogs, tadpoles, and mice.
- Spiders are found in most areas of the world. They live wherever food is available.
- There are over 30,000 known kinds of spiders. However, some scientists believe there may be as many as 100,000 types.
- Spiders can be as large as a person's hand or be smaller than the head of a pin.
- Spiders can be grouped according to their way of life: hunting spiders lie in wait or run after their prey. Web-spinning spiders spin webs to attract their prey.

Scripture Links
- The deeds of evildoers are compared to a spider's webs (Isaiah 59:5–6).

Let's Explore!
Spider Safari
Take a field trip to a wooded area or search vegetation for spider webs, preferably in the early morning when webs may be covered with dew. Bring magnifying glasses, a misting bottle filled with water, notebooks, and pencils. Since some spiders are poisonous, warn students not to touch the spiders or webs. Once a web is located, observe it for any activity. Are any insects caught in the web? Is the spider nearby? Look for an abandoned web. Squirt it gently with the spray bottle. Use magnifying glasses to investigate webs more closely. Draw the spider webs. Use the Internet or other resources to see if you can identify your spider from its web.

Spider and Web Art
Draw a spider web on a 9" x 12" (22.8 cm x 30.5 cm) piece of white paper. Place a 12" piece of waxed paper over the drawing. Trace the web with white glue. Sprinkle silver glitter over the glue and let dry. To make a spider, fold a 3-inch square of black paper in

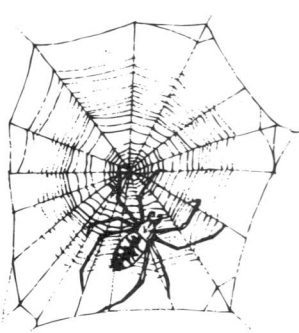

The Spinning Spider (cont.)

half. On the fold, draw half of the spider's body. Cut out and add eyes and fangs. Trim the excess paper around the web. Tape a knotted piece of gray or white yarn to the back of the spider. Poke a small hole in the web and push the other end of the yarn through to the back of the web. Knot and tape it to the back of the web. Hang to display.

Ode to a Spider

Many people fear spiders. Encourage children to use the creativity God gave them and compose a song, write a poem, design a poster, or write a paragraph detailing how spiders are our friends.

Poison Spider Game

For this game, enlarge and make two copies of the spider below. Copy one spider on green and one on red paper. Decorate as desired, cut out, and laminate. Tape or glue a large craft stick to the back of each spider. Cut several spider webs from black or gray construction paper. If desired, use the web on page 30. Write letters or numbers on the spider webs and then laminate them for durability. Tape the spider webs randomly on the floor.

To play "Poison Spider," have one child be the spider and the other children be fish, birds, turtles, or snakes. Have the spider's predators line up on one side of the room while the spider stands on the opposite side with his back to them. When the spider holds up the green spider, the predators must move quietly from one spider web to the next across the room and try to tag the spider. The spider can, at any time, hold up the red spider and turn around quickly to see if he can catch any predators moving. If he does, the spider must direct the predator to return to a specified spider web. Continue playing until the spider is tagged. The child who tags the spider becomes the new spider and play begins again.

Long I Collage

Enlarge, copy, and cut out several spiders from the pattern. Color and then glue the spiders to a large sheet of construction paper. In groups or by themselves, have students search magazines to find pictures of things that have the long i sound. Cut out and glue the pictures onto the construction paper around the spiders to make a Long I Collage. Have students write or dictate the words they find underneath each picture. Display the collages for parents, teachers, and students to enjoy.

A Tangram Spider

Enlarge, copy, and cut out the tangrams on page 31. Make three or four copies for each student. Or make one copy and have the students cut out the tangrams and trace onto construction paper to make multiple copies of each shape. Have each student create his or her own spider using only the tangram pieces. Glue the spider onto a large piece of butcher block or construction paper web.

Name _____

A Web of Facts

Research a type of spider, such as the black widow or wolf spider. Write the spider's name in the center of the web. Then complete the web by filling in the spaces with facts about that spider. Draw a picture of your spider on the web.

Tangrams

My Insect Award

_____
(Name)

has successfully learned about insects in the Bible!